21st Century
Junior Library

INFOGRAPHICS:
SHAPE OF THE GAME

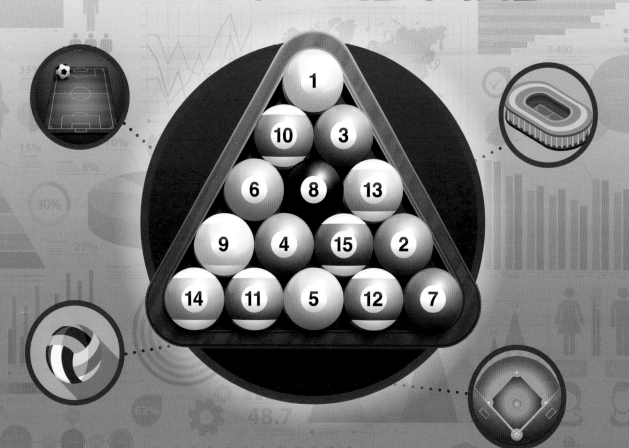

Sports-Graphics Jr.

Heather Williams

Published in the United States of America by:

CHERRY LAKE PRESS
2395 South Huron Parkway, Suite 200, Ann Arbor, Michigan 48104
www.cherrylakepress.com

Reading Adviser: Beth Walker Gambro, MS, Ed., Reading Consultant, Yorkville, IL

Photo Credits: © Praewpalilin/Getty Images, © bortonia/Getty Images, © elinedesignservices/Getty Images, © Rvector/Shutterstock, cover; © Jessica Orozco, © XonkArts/Getty Images, © EgudinKa/Getty Images, 5; © Jessica Orozco, © Roman Prysiazhniuk/Getty Images, 7; © Jessica Orozco, 8; © Jessica Orozco, 9; © Jessica Orozco, 11; © biolalabet/Shutterstock, © Brovko Serhii/Shutterstock, © Jessica Orozco, 12; © GoodStudio/Shutterstock, © Top Vector Studio/Shutterstock, © Paragorn Dangsombroon/Shutterstock, © JuliarStudio/Getty Images, 14; © Pretty Vectors/Shutterstock, ©freehandz/Getty Images, 15; © Jessica Orozco, 16; © DoggieMonkey/Getty Images, © apagafonova/Getty Images, © Ihor Reshetniak/Getty Images, © FishDesigns/Getty Images, 17; © grimgram/Getty Images, © Belliely/Getty Images, 20; © kup1984/Getty Images, ©djvstock/Getty Images, 21s

Cherry Lake Press is an imprint of Cherry Lake Publishing Group.

Library of Congress Cataloging-in-Publication Data has been filed and is available at catalog.loc.gov.

Cherry Lake Publishing Group would like to acknowledge the work of the Partnership for 21st Century Learning, a Network of Battelle for Kids. Please visit Battelle for Kids online for more information.

Printed in the United States of America

Note from publisher: Websites change regularly, and their future contents are outside of our control. Supervise children when conducting any recommended online searches for extended learning opportunities.

ABOUT THE AUTHOR

Heather Williams is a former English teacher and school librarian. She has a passion for seeing readers of all ages connect with others through stories and experiences. Heather has written more than 50 books for children. She enjoys walking her dog, reading, and watching sports. She lives in North Carolina with her husband and two children.

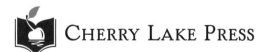

CONTENTS

SHAPES IN SPORTS

Athletes need rules when they play sports. Rules make the game fair. Some rules are about the **area** of the field or court. Some are about the equipment used. That's where shapes come in handy. Sports rules cover shapes and dimensions. All basketball games are played on a rectangle-shaped court. Courts are the same size for each age group. Other sports have similar rules. This gives teams an equal playing field.

BASIC SPORTS SHAPES

SPHERE

A sphere is round and solid. This shape has no edges.

RHOMBUS

A rhombus is a four-sided shape. It has four equal, straight sides. The angles of opposite corners are the same.

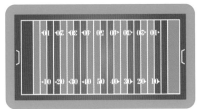

RECTANGLE

A rectangle is a four-sided shape. It has four right angles. Two sides are usually longer than the other two sides. (Squares are an exception. They have four equal sides.)

TRIANGLE

A triangle is a three-sided shape. Its angles add up to 180°.

MULTISPORT DIMENSIONS

Most goal sports take place on a rectangle. Goal sports include basketball, football, and soccer. The goal is the focus of the game. This is how teams score. There is a goal on each end of the field or court. Courts and fields are longer on the sides. They have four equal corners. They are all 90° angles. Having goals on the short ends makes scoring and defending the goals easier. Straight lines and corners also create clear **boundaries**.

COURT DIMENSIONS

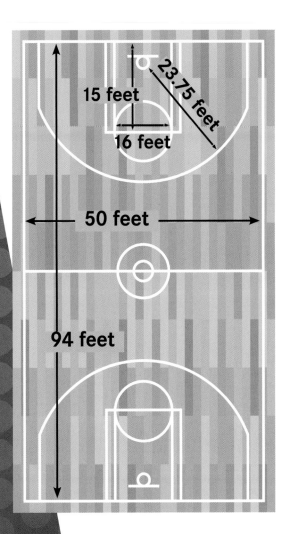

BASKETBALL COURTS

- National Basketball Association (NBA), Women's National Basketball Association (WNBA), and National Collegiate Athletic Association (NCAA) basketball courts are the same size. They measure 94 x 50 feet (29 x 15 meters).

- High school basketball courts are 84 x 50 feet (26 x 15 m).

- Middle school courts are 74 x 42 feet (23 x 13 m).

SOCCER PITCH SHAPES

Soccer fields are different sizes. The size depends on the age of the players and the number of people on each team. Professional fields can be anywhere from 100 to 130 yards (91 to 119 m) long and 50 to 100 yards (46 to 91 m) wide. Youth soccer fields are smaller.

FIELD A:
YOUTH
4 AGAINST 4

FIELD B:
YOUTH
7 AGAINST 7

FIELD C:
YOUTH
9 AGAINST 9

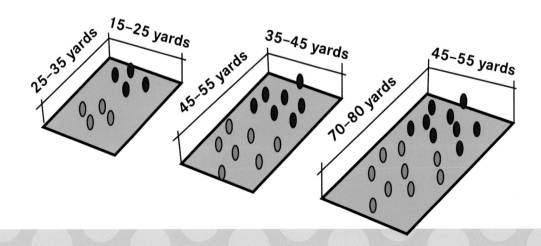

THE BASEBALL FIELD

A polygon is a shape with three or more sides.
How many polygons are on a baseball field?

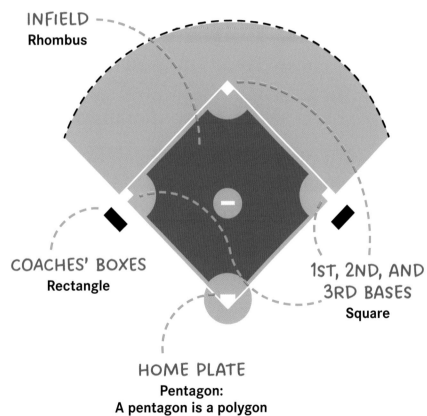

INFIELD
Rhombus

COACHES' BOXES
Rectangle

1ST, 2ND, AND
3RD BASES
Square

HOME PLATE
**Pentagon:
A pentagon is a polygon
with five sides.**

GAMETIME GEOMETRY

Area is how long and how wide a shape is. But some shapes in sports are **three-dimensional** (3D). Swimming pools are one example. The pool is filled with water. It takes up space in all directions. Rules in swimming determine the length and width of the pool. They also cover depth. Hockey games take place on a flat surface. It looks a lot like a basketball court. But hockey is played on ice. The ice must have a certain thickness to support the players.

THE ICE IS RIGHT

Hockey is played on a rectangle. Five face-off circles are painted onto the ice.

NATIONAL HOCKEY LEAGUE (NHL) RINK

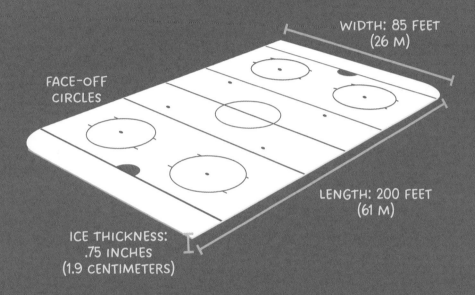

WIDTH: 85 FEET (26 M)

FACE-OFF CIRCLES

LENGTH: 200 FEET (61 M)

ICE THICKNESS: .75 INCHES (1.9 CENTIMETERS)

The ice on a hockey rink is made of around 64 layers of frozen water. Calculate the volume of the ice with this formula:

(length x width x depth) x 7.5 = volume
(200 x 85 x 0.0625 feet) x 7.5 = volume
(1062.5) x 7.5 = 7,968.75 gallons

SPORTS CYLINDERS

A **cylinder** is a round 3D shape. Cylinders have a top and bottom that are circular. The pole that holds up a football goalpost is a cylinder. Some basketball goals are held up by a cylinder. Items used to play sports can also be cylinder-shaped.

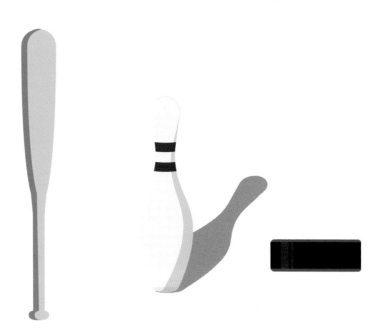

BASEBALL BAT
34 inches (86 cm) x
2.6 inches (6.6 cm)

BOWLING PIN
15 inches (38 cm) x
2 inches (5 cm)

HOCKEY PUCK
1 inch (2.5 cm) x
3 inches (7.6 cm)

SHAPE-SHIFTING THE GAME

Sometimes people see a way to make the sport better. Then the rules change. New technology has helped make soccer balls better. Their shape has changed. They are made of better materials. Stadiums have also changed. They come in many sizes and shapes. Some stadiums are for many sports. Others are made for just one sport.

SHAPES OF STADIUMS

Panathenaic Stadium, 330 BCE

Rectangular with rounded corners; "stadium" is actually the name of a shape. It means a rectangle with rounded ends.

Colosseum in Rome, 80 CE

The Colosseum is called the "father of modern stadiums." It has high walls with rows of seating around an oval playing field.

Lord's Cricket Ground, 1812

The first grandstand was built in the early 1800s. Grandstands have long rectangular rows of covered seats. They overlook a cricket or soccer field.

Harvard Stadium, 1903

Harvard Stadium is the oldest still-used concrete stadium in the United States. It is shaped like a U or horseshoe.

White City Stadium, 1908
The first oval-shaped stadium with seating areas in the curved parts was built in the early 1900s.

Astrodome, 1965
The Astrodome was the first fully covered oval-shaped stadium.

SkyDome Toronto, 1989
The first retractable roof oval-shaped stadium was built in Canada.

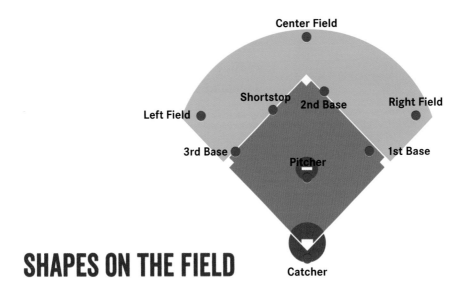

SHAPES ON THE FIELD

People create shapes in sports, too. Each player on a team has a **position**. First, all of the players get into their positions. Then they make a shape called a **formation**. Some sports have several formations. Others have just one or two. In baseball, the **outfield** positions are always the same. In soccer, there are many different formations.

PICKLEBALL VS. TENNIS

Pickleball is similar to tennis. It is played on a smaller court with slightly different equipment.

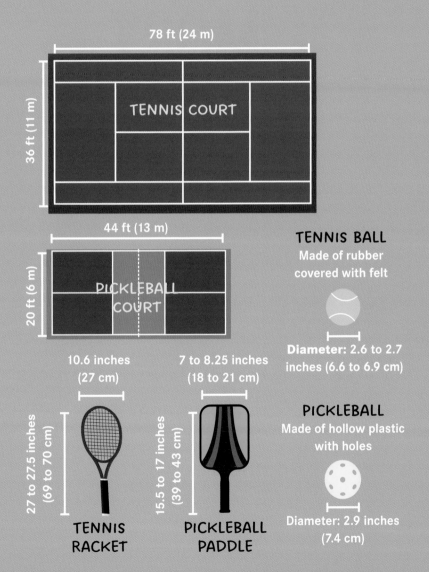

78 ft (24 m)

36 ft (11 m)

TENNIS COURT

44 ft (13 m)

20 ft (6 m)

PICKLEBALL COURT

TENNIS BALL
Made of rubber covered with felt

Diameter: 2.6 to 2.7 inches (6.6 to 6.9 cm)

10.6 inches (27 cm)

7 to 8.25 inches (18 to 21 cm)

PICKLEBALL
Made of hollow plastic with holes

Diameter: 2.9 inches (7.4 cm)

27 to 27.5 inches (69 to 70 cm)

15.5 to 17 inches (39 to 43 cm)

TENNIS RACKET

PICKLEBALL PADDLE

FIRST, BEST, MOST

Every sport has a first game. The first Olympics took place about 3,000 years ago. The first baseball game was in 1846. Pickleball and snowboarding were invented in the 1960s.

No matter how old or new, every sport has records. Records tell which runner can race around the oval shape of the track the fastest. They list the players who have hit the most spherical balls out of a baseball stadium. Some records are about how big a stadium is or how many balls are used in a game.

HOW MANY BALLS DOES IT TAKE?

Players go through a lot of spheres and cylinders during a typical game. By the end of a regular season, the numbers can really add up! Take a look at how many balls and pucks are used in the four major U.S. pro sports leagues each season.

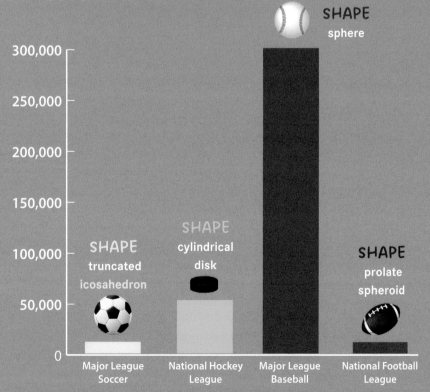

SHAPE
sphere

SHAPE
truncated
icosahedron

SHAPE
cylindrical
disk

SHAPE
prolate
spheroid

300,000			
250,000			
200,000			
150,000			
100,000			
50,000			
0			

Major League Soccer | National Hockey League | Major League Baseball | National Football League

UNIQUE SHAPES AND UNUSUAL LOCATIONS

HONISTER SLATE MINE

Cumbria, England
World's first underground cricket match, played in 2013
to raise money for a team's flooded cricket grounds;
match was played 2,000 feet (610 m)
below ground

Rectangular mesh pitch

THE FLOAT

Marina Bay, Singapore
World's largest
floating stadium

Rectangle

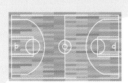

CARRIER CLASSIC, U.S.S. *CARL VINSON*

San Diego, California
First basketball game played on an aircraft carrier between Michigan
State and the University of North Carolina, November 11, 2011; stan-
dard wooden basketball court was constructed on the carrier's flight
deck, which is 252 feet (77 m) wide and has a total area of
4.5 acres (1.8 hectares)

Rectangle

NATIONAL AQUATICS CENTER

Beijing, China

Built for the 2008 Olympics; largest ETFE-covered structure in the world
(ETFE is a type of plastic that allows more natural light and heat than
glass); 584 x 584 x 102 feet (178 x 178 x 31.1 m)

Three-dimensional rectangular cuboid

RUNGRADO 1ST OF MAY STADIUM

Pyongyang, North Korea

Largest stadium in the world;
seats 150,000 people

Circular, shaped like an
open parachute

BURJ AL ARAB HELIPAD TENNIS COURT

Dubai, United Arab Emirates

World's highest tennis court; a match was played there between Roger
Federer and Andre Agassi in 2005; 1,503 feet (458 m) high

Circle

ACTIVITY

Shaping New Rules of the Game

Cricket is one of the few sports with a playing field that can have many different shapes and sizes. But what if you changed the size and shape of a basketball court? What if tennis balls were bigger? Pick a sport and make big changes to it by changing the shapes it uses.

Materials Needed

- Paper or poster board
- Writing utensil

1. First, choose a sport. Make sure you understand how the game is already played. This will make it easier to create your own rules.

2. Make a drawing of the field or court. Include basic equipment.

3. Reimagine the playing area. Consider using unique shapes such as triangles and hexagons. Make a sketch.

4. Next, decide what you will change about the equipment. Draw your ideas.

5. Now, make new rules based on the above changes. Will there be more bases? More goals? Will you need more players?

6. Finally, try out your new game! How did your changes affect gameplay?

FIND OUT MORE

Books

Hawkes, Chris. *My Encyclopedia of Very Important Sports.* New York: DK Publishing, 2020.

Stark, Kristy. *Fields, Rinks, and Courts: Partitioning Shapes.* Huntington Beach, CA: Teacher Created Materials, 2018.

Online Resources to Explore with an Adult

Kiddle: Sport Facts for Kids

Soccer Training Lab: The Ultimate Guide to Soccer Formations

YouTube: "Geometric Shapes [Science of NFL Football]"

Bibliography

Dimensions. "Sports Equipment."

Dimensions. "Sports Fields."

Schrag, Miles. *The Sports Rules Book.* Champaign, IL: Human Kinetics, 2019.

GLOSSARY

area (AIR-ee-uh) the amount of space inside of a flat shape

boundaries (BOWN-duh-reez) things that show where one area ends and another area begins

cylinder (SIL-uhn-duhr) a shape with straight sides and two circular ends, like a tube

diameter (dye-AM-uh-tuhr) the length between two opposite points of a circle

dimensions (duh-MEN-shuhns) the measurements of a shape or object, such as length and width

formations (for-MAY-shuns) in sports, a way that players are arranged on courts or fields

icosahedron (ahy-koh-suh-HEE-druhn) a ball-like shape with 20 sides

outfield (OWT-feeld) the area past the central playing space in baseball

position (puh-ZIH-shuhn) in sports, the job a player has on a team

rectangular cuboid (rek-TAYNG-yoo-lur KYOO-boyd) three-dimensional shape that has 6 rectangular sides, 12 edges, and 8 right angles

three-dimensional (three-duh-MEN-shuh-nuhl) a shape or space that has height, length, and depth

INDEX